M.A.D.E.

(Mothers and Daughters Excel)

In Him

A Small Group Bible Study Series

BRENDA S. GIBSON

ISBN-13: 978-0692652800

This book is dedicated with love
to Laney and Gracey
who have consistently given me
plenty to pray about.
I love you girls!

CONTENTS

Acknowledgments

Thank you to my family, friends and fellow writers who encouraged me along the way through prayers, mentoring and words of endorsement.

I'm especially grateful to the Florida Christian Writers Conference of 2015 and the fellow writers who inspired and encouraged me with prayers and practical advice. Thanks for giving me a real sense of camaraderie.

Hugs to my dear friend Kathie Z. for countless hours of long walks, poignant prayers, late night phone calls and cheering me on.

A special note to Bishop L., Jean W. and Jim L. for allowing me to bend your ear over a quick cup of coffee or breakfast. I truly admire all of you and the gracious way you are willing to listen and mentor. I appreciate it!

A big thanks to my mom and dad who planted the seed of faith in me when I was a child and have walked alongside me in faith ever since. They are always ready to lend a hand . . . . I love you both so dearly.

Thank you to my girls, Laney and Gracey—for helping me see that I will always be your mom no matter what and realizing there's nothing you can do about it—makes me smile! I love you both so much.

To my husband, Chris, thank you for always being here for me and supporting all my endeavors. I want everyone to know that I'm proud of our 30+ years of marriage. You continue to be God's gift in my life and there's no one I'd rather have by my side on this journey. I love you always.

Most importantly, to God for placing this idea on my heart so many years ago—thank you for your gentle nudges when I get off track and your loving Spirit within me who is my source of strength and power, now and forever.

What This Book Is About

M.A.D.E. in Him was developed specifically for middle school girls and their mothers. The study includes twelve easy-to-follow hourly sessions for small groups of mothers and daughters. The layout makes it easy for anyone to facilitate, and the best part is the study has been tried, tested, and proven to work! Special features also included: Leader's Notes, Session Extenders and Day Retreat Ideas.

Mothers and daughters share a unique relationship with each other . . .

We need to make sure we create a safe environment for our daughters to tell us anything and to let them know we are there for them. We can accomplish this by simply being ready to talk and/or listen at any given moment. When we make ourselves available, we convey their importance to us and our love for them. When our time together is founded in a love for Christ, this relationship – as confidantes, best friends, and parent-child – has the power to excel beyond imagination!

"A great way to create a closer mother-daughter bond through faith!"

Introduction

From the very first treat made in her "Easy-Bake-Oven," our older daughter hosted little tea parties, first with an assortment of stuffed animals and then for her baby sister when she was able to sit up. By age 6, she had hosted several parties that I was invited to as well.

During her elementary years, invitations to birthday parties replaced the tea parties. These were usually drop off parties where the parents trusted the host families to care for their children for the duration of the party. I made sure I always knew something about the family before just dropping off my girls, however, that wasn't a guarantee that things wouldn't go wrong at the party.

As our older daughter entered middle school, I felt the need to revisit the tea party idea but with a grown up twist. She was heading toward the high school years, with their own unique challenges, so I wanted us to reconnect and to let her know I would always be here for her. Not wanting to go it alone, I contacted other mothers and daughters to organize regular get-togethers. Our first mother-daughter tea party was held one Sunday afternoon in my home. Then we met monthly for over a year.

At each monthly get-together, we addressed challenges and issues from a Christian perspective and explored our faith together in a safe and honest environment. It was a wonderful time to form close relationships with each other and to gain the support of other mothers and daughters. After each meeting, I created an outline for a study and noticed what went well and how we could make the most of this time together.

My daughters are now young adults, but I always knew at some point I wanted to share this idea with other moms! It's a great way to create a closer mother-daughter bond through faith.

When you honor your relationships, you honor God . . . and you will be blessed and be a blessing to others!

These commandments that I give you today are to be on your hearts. Impress them on your children. Talk about them when you sit at home and when you walk along the road, when you lie down and when you get up.

Deuteronomy 6:6-7

Session 1

Finding True Love Today . . .

Love is patient, love is kind. Its does not envy, it does not boast, it is not proud. It does not dishonor others, it is not self-seeking, it is not easily angered, it keeps no record of wrongs. Love does not delight in evil but rejoices with the truth. It always protects, always trusts, always hopes always perseveres.

1 Corinthians 13:4-6

Session Overview

As Christians, we are called to love one another, but what does that really mean? As we consider the word "LOVE" and what it truly means to love one another and to be loved, we'll compare and contrast what scripture has to say. We'll also look at how spending time together is important in building and maintaining healthy relationships.

What You'll Need

- Bible
- Journal
- Paper and pens for everyone
- Craft supplies (Extending the Session)

Opening Prayer

Dear Lord,
Thank You for this time You have set aside for us to be together today, so we may hear Your Word and gather an understanding about our relationship with You, our family, friends, and the world around us. Open our hearts and minds that we may experience a fun and fulfilling session.
In Your Name We Pray, Amen

Opening Activity

"Who Knew?"

Moms and daughters, "How well do you know each other?" Sometimes knowing a little something about another person, can help you understand her a little better. Spending more time with someone can help as well. First, let's find out what you do know about each other.

Just for fun!

Answer the following questions about each other and write them down on a separate piece of paper. When all the questions are answered, exchange papers and count up the number of correct answers.

Take a moment to share the answers about each other. You may be surprised!

1) What's her favorite color?

2) What's her shoe size?

3) Who's her favorite singer?

4) What's her favorite season?

5) What's her favorite snack?

6) What's her favorite song?

7) If she could travel anywhere in the world, where would that be?

8) Between a book or a movie, what would she choose?

"Did You Know?..."

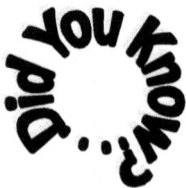

Communication, trust, respect and love are key ingredients in creating and maintaining healthy relationships.

Let's Talk . . .

Consider the words from 1 Corinthians 13:4-6. Notice the passage begins with what love is and then goes into what it is not.

Let's make a comparison chart: **What Love Is vs. What Love Is Not** according to the scripture. *(Hint: Rephrase some in your own words.)*

LOVE Is . . .	Versus	LOVE Is Not . . .
_____		_____
_____		_____
_____		_____
_____		_____
_____		_____

1) Take a look at your chart. What stands out to you in comparison?

2) What is love, in your own words?

3) Think about the phrase "It always protects, always trusts, always hopes, always perseveres." How does that make you feel?

Now consider God's love for us . . .

For God so loved the world that he gave his one and only Son, that whoever believes in him shall not perish but have eternal life. For God did not send his Son into the world to condemn the world, but to save the world through him.

- John 3:16-17

Through God's love for us, we are given Jesus Christ, His Son, who is sent to this world to save us and teach us. This kind of love shows patience with a world that had become corrupt. What an amazing love!

We also know that God's love: "Always protects, always trusts, always hopes, always perseveres." It should make us feel special and safe to know that He is always here for us!

Love for your family is a special love that creates a safe place to try new things and to talk over ideas with each other. When we practice patience, kindness, and trust with each other, we create a closer mother-daughter bond through faith.

As we explore the Bible together, consider what God says about love. What do you want your relationships to reflect: patience, kindness, trust?

A Treasure for Your Thoughts

Consider the following memory verse, and rewrite it in your own words.

Your Memory Treasure . . . .

The fear of the Lord is the beginning of
knowledge, but fools despise wisdom
and discipline.

In Your Own Words:

Your Creative Space:

Design a Bookmark based on the Proverbs verse.

Journal Your Thoughts

Take a moment to write down your thoughts about today's session.
Here are a few ideas to help you get started:

1. We learned how God defines love, but how does the world around us define love? *(Hint: Include some examples)*
2. List some ways you can show love for your family today.
3. Always include a list of things you appreciate . . . It's uplifting!

Closing Prayer

Dear Lord,
Thank You for showing us what love is and what love is not. Continue to help us show love for You and for each other, so our relationships are built on a strong foundation based on love and respect.
Thank You for this beautiful and unique mother-daughter relationship.
May it bring glory to Your name and be a light in this world.
In Your Name We Pray,
Amen

Prayer Request

Are there people in your group who need extra prayers? Is there a world concern that needs to be prayed for? Record them here and pray throughout the week.

A Mother's Reflection . . . . Shared by Jeanie W.

I witnessed Love this week. I watched my daughter Katie holding her newborn baby, Kyla. With protective arms supporting the infant's still wobbly head, Katie smiled and hummed a quiet tune. It was like no one else was in the room. Their eyes, fixated on one another, radiated an intense love.

I, a mere creature, a human, can never fully comprehend how much God loves us. Yet when I observed this tender and adoring exchange between a mother and child, I caught a glimpse of the Divine.

"Listen to me...you whom I have upheld since you were conceived, and have carried since your birth. Even to your old age and gray hairs I am he, I am he who will sustain you. I have made you and I will carry you; I will sustain you and I will rescue you."
- Isaiah 46:3-4

Throughout our earthly journey, God continues to hold each of us in His protective arms, supporting our wobbly fears. Like a baby's full reliance on a mother's care, our faith rests in his promise to watch over us.

"As a mother comforts her child, so I will comfort you."　　　**- Isaiah 66:13**

As Katie's face glowed with a tender smile, I just knew God also smiles when he watches us. He "beholds" us, giving us His full attention. God knows the full plan so can easily smile even during our difficulties – He knows our journey will end – once again in His arms.

"He will rejoice over you with singing."　　　**- Zephaniah 3:17**

I wonder what song God sings to us as He holds us tenderly in His strong arms. Just think: the God who never lets us go, also sings over us. What beautiful music that must be.

Who does the baby hear when a mother hums a quiet lullaby? Maybe Kyla can still hear God's joyous melody enfolding her heart. I watched my daughter Katie, holding her newborn baby, Kyla. I witnessed Love.

Session 2

Finding Yourself
in a Selfish World . . .

For you created my inmost being; you knit me together in my mother's womb.
I praise you because I am fearfully and wonderfully made.

Psalm 139: 13-14

Session Overview

How do you see yourself? We are bombarded daily with countless images in magazines, commercials, reality shows and social media, which are all devoted to telling us how to be our "best self" or get the "best look" . . . no wonder it's hard to imagine that God created us perfectly just the way we are!

We'll explore how unique we are through God's eyes.

What You'll Need

- Bible
- Journal
- Paper and pens for everyone
- Craft supplies (Extending the Session)

Opening Prayer

Dear Lord,

Thank You for gathering us today. Help us focus on how You created us as "One of a Kind" in this world and to know we are in a safe place to share our own thoughts and ideas with each other.

In Your Name We Pray,

Amen

Opening Activity

"What's on Your Mind?"
We spend a good portion of our days listening, watching, and even interacting with all sorts of communication devices.
What sort of things are you watching and listening to that consume a good part of your time?

Take a moment to write and share your favorite . . .

TV Show_____

Song _____

Movie _____

Social Media _____

Magazine _____

Now consider these questions for a moment:

1. "What images, behaviors, or lyrics are some of your listed favorites conveying?"

2. Are they filled with uplifting and positive messages that you can use in your daily life?

3. Does it matter what we view, watch or listen to?

Did You Know?...

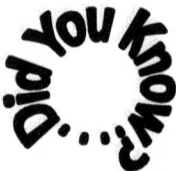

Images stick with you long after you see them. Your mind recalls the images and they will have an impact on you... Good or bad!

Let's Talk . . .

Consider the words in Psalm 139:13-14.

1) What do these words mean?

   "Because I am fearfully and wonderfully made"

2) What do you think about God knitting us together in your mother's womb?

   What does that imply?

3) Knowing that God created you, just the way you are . . .

   How does that make you feel?

We are wonderfully made and created for purpose . . .

† *For we are God's handiwork, created in Christ Jesus to do good works, which God prepared in advance for us to do.*

- Ephesians 2:10

1) What are we considered as?

2) What are we created for?

3) How unique and special do you feel now?

We are God's special work of art and the very God that created us wants peace and joy for us. We can rest in knowing that we were created to do God's work and being a positive light in this world that is sometimes filled with darkness.

One of a Kind is how God created us and seeing ourselves through God's eyes will always reveal just how wonderfully made we are. He created each of us in a unique way and with a unique purpose.

As your relationship with God grows, you will see yourself as God intended -- wonderfully made and fully capable of being yourself -- even in a world full of images!

A Treasure for Your Thoughts

Consider the following memory verse, and rewrite it in your own words.

Your Memory Treasure . . . .

The discerning heart seeks knowledge,
but the mouth of a fool feeds on folly.
Proverbs 15:14

In Your Own Words:

Your Creative Space:

Design a Bumper Sticker based on the Proverbs verse.

Journal Your Thoughts

Take a moment to write down your thoughts about today's session.
Here are a few ideas to help you get started:

1. We learned just how special we are in God's eyes, so how does that make you feel?
2. List some ways you can show others how special they are.
3. What do you like about yourself?

Closing Prayer

Dear Lord,
Thank You for creating us just the way we are. Continue to help us seek You daily and look to You for guidance so we are not caught up in worldly images.
Thank you for this beautiful and unique mother-daughter relationship.
May it bring glory to Your name and be a light in this world.
In Your Name We Pray,
Amen

Prayer Requests

Are there people in your group who need extra prayers? Is there a world concern that needs to be prayed for? Record them here and pray throughout the week.

A Mother's Reflection . . . . Shared by Amy R.

I was blessed to be raised by a very loving, giving, faith-filled mom who honestly and patiently answered my questions, always put her family first and taught me the importance of relying on God as my source of strength and hope. All of this provided me a strong foundation on which to build my role as a mother when my daughter was born.

Like my mom and I, my daughter and I "get" one another. We share similar personality traits and thought patterns. These likenesses afford us a special bond of closeness not every mother/daughter duo can experience. I treasure this bond with my daughter and respect its preciousness every moment of every day.

As I have witnessed my daughter's blossoming faith and deepening relationship with the Lord, I am in awe of her wisdom and conviction. I believe her honesty and innocence is a gift from God, and I am thankful to Him for the privilege of being her mom. It is in that role where I have a front row seat to her development into a young woman of and for God.

> *I treasure this bond with my daughter and respect its preciousness every moment of every day.*

Session 3

Family Support . . .

But as for me and my household, we will serve the Lord.

Joshua 24:15

Session Overview

Families will experience all sorts of ups and downs throughout life. We'll look at biblical ways families can support each other in good times and rough times and how families were created to serve the Lord. We'll also look at how spending time together is important for building a trusting home.

What You'll Need

- Bible
- Journal
- Colored markers or pencils for everyone (6 different colors)
- Craft supplies (Extending the Session)

Opening Prayer

Dear Lord,
Thank You for our families and the friends we have surrounded ourselves with today. Help us to create a place of support for each other. Open our hearts and minds that we may experience a fun and fulfilling session.
In Your Name We Pray,
Amen

Opening Activity

"Where Does the Time Go?"
Have you heard the expression "Time flies"? On busy days, time flies and goes too fast! So how do you spend your time on a daily basis?
Use the guide below to fill in the chart with the coordinating color:
RED- Time with friends, taking care of pets, helping others
GREEN- Playing sports, exercising, reading, playing/listening to music
ORANGE- School, homework
PURPLE- Video games, social media, texting, watching TV
YELLOW- Praying, Bible Study, Church
BLUE- Chores, sleeping, eating, getting ready

Time	Mon.	Tues.	Wed.	Thurs.	Fri.	Sat.	Sun.
7:00am							
8:00							
9:00							
10:00							
11:00							
12pm							
1:00							
2:00							
3:00							
4:00							
5:00							
6:00							
7:00							
8:00							
9:00							
10:00							
11:00							
12am							

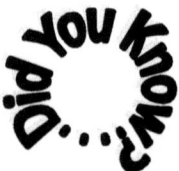

Did you know?...

How we choose to spend our time directly affects our mind, body and spirit.

Let's Talk . . .

Consider the words in Joshua 24:15.

1) What does the phrase mean? *"As for me and my household"*

2) What do you think is meant by *"We will serve the Lord"*?

3) What are ways to serve the Lord as a family?

Your family just got bigger . . .

The Spirit himself testifies with our spirit that we are God's children.
— **Romans 8:16**

1) Who is the first "Spirit" this verse refers to?

2) If we are all God's children, what does that make us?

3) What do you think it means to be a sister in Christ?

Because we are sisters in Christ, your family just got bigger! We are connected through God our Father who gave us Jesus Christ and empowered us with His Holy Spirit. That should make you feel great, because as you look around this room today, you can call each other family!

God created people to fulfill the need for human companionship. Living together as a family is a wonderful opportunity to create an environment to grow in faith and love for Christ and each other. Spending time together is essential for bonding and learning how to support each other in good times and rough times.

A Treasure for Your Thoughts

Consider the following memory verse, and rewrite it in your own words.

Your Memory Treasure . . . .

He who brings trouble on his family
will inherit only wind.
Proverbs 15:14

In Your Own Words:

Your Creative Space:

Design a Button based on the Proverbs verse.

Journal Your Thoughts

Take a moment to write down your thoughts about today's session.
Here are a few ideas to help you get started:
1. We learned that we are sisters in Christ. What does that really mean to you?
2. List some ways you can spend time with your family.
3. What are some things you like about family?

Closing Prayer

Dear Lord,
Thank You for creating us to be family. Help us grow in love and care for each other just as You have taught us to do in the Bible. May we always enjoy the times we spend together.
Thank You for this beautiful and unique mother-daughter relationship.
May it bring glory to Your name and be a light in this world.
In Your Name We Pray,
Amen

Prayer Requests

Are there people in your group who need extra prayers? Is there a world concern that needs to be prayed for? Record them here and pray throughout the week.

A Mother's Reflection . . . . Shared by Julie I.

As life gets busy with activities for our children, it's also hectic for moms too. BUT, I try to make my children a priority and they know it. I sit and listen to my girls at any moment they need me. I drop whatever I'm doing and listen. They often need advice about a friend, teacher or situation. It's an honor to be recognized as worthy in my teenager's eyes and to be asked for counseling and guidance. During these precarious years, I'm honored my girls' trust me to know what's going on in their lives and they include me in their inner circle.

We have the grace to laugh at each other and with each other. We have fun together! We enjoy being together. Many of our fondest memories thus far are around the dinner table. Yes, I try to make time for dinner as a family. Do we eat at 5:00? No, dinner comes at all times in the evening, but typically after 7:30. Do we want to eat at 8:00? No, but often this is when everyone is home at the same time. I feel it's important to sit together as a family and bond. We share details about our day, learn about one another, and contribute to the central family conversation. During our time together we continue to grow as a family unit bonding with silliness, problem-solving and encouragement.

The relationship I have with my daughters is one of the biggest blessings in my life. I am so thankful God has given me the privilege to be their mom, confidant, and friend.

Beautiful quotes by Patsy Zant:

- The very special bond between mother and daughter is the one place in all the world where hearts can be sure of each other.
- Like branches on a tree, we may grow in different directions, but our roots remain one.
- And through the fury of the storm or the calm of the rainbow, we depend on each other for understanding and compassion.

Session 4

Finding Good Friends . . .

Two are better than one, because they have a good return for their work: If one falls down, his friend can help him up. But pity the man who falls and has no one to help him up!

Joshua 24:15

Session Overview

In a world filled with all kinds of influences, good and bad, how do we find friends that are good influencers? How do we become a good influence? We'll look at what makes a good friend and how to be a good friend.

What You'll Need

- Bible
- Journal
- Craft supplies (Extending the Session)

Opening Prayer

Dear Lord,
Thank You for gathering us here today to have fun and experience Your Word as we explore friendship. Help us learn to be a good friend to one another and support each other in our faith. Open our hearts and minds to hear Your Word.
In Your Name We Pray,
Amen

Opening Activity

"Friends?"

Sometimes what draws us to people are the things we share in common such as activities, religion, mutual friends, where we live and so on. We choose friends for all sorts of reasons, but do you really know what kind of friend you like or what kind of friend you'd like to be? Let's think for a moment.

Daughters:

Take turns around the room to answer the following question out loud: "If your mom was the same age you are now, would you be friends?" Why or why not? *(Be as open and honest as you can.)*

If we recognize that common interests can bring friendships together, we should also recognize that opposite interests can bring friendships together as well. How can this be? Sometimes opposites balance each other out and give us another point of view. If we were all exactly the same, it would be a boring world and nothing would change.

Let's take a moment to make a list of at least seven qualities you think are important in a friend and be ready to discuss why.
A good friend is . . .

1)

2)

3)

4)

5)

6)

7)

Did you know?...

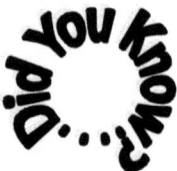

Good friends will make you feel good about yourself and you will want to be around them.

Let's Talk

Consider the words from Ecclesiastes 4:9-10. The passage begins: *"Two are better than one."*

Finish reading the passage and fill in the missing words or phrases:

"If one _____, his friend can _____."

"But pity the man who falls and has _____!"

Answer the following questions:

1) What do you think "Two are better than one" means?

2) Why pity someone who has no one to help him up?

3) What does this say about the importance of a good friend?

The friends you make and keep are important.

Walk with the wise and become wise, for a companion of fools suffers harm.
– Proverbs 13:20

There is an old saying, "One bad apple spoils the barrel," which means the one apple can ruin everything around it. Who we choose as our friends does matter, because they influence us good or bad. The more time we spend with them, the more we become like them. It is important to ask yourself: "Are you a good influence on your friends and are your friends a good influence on you?" Do you hold each other accountable?

Finding Good Friends is more about being a good friend. Being kind, trustworthy and dependable will help you find those special kind of friends that stick by you no matter what.

When we work on building our relationships, we honor each other and in doing so, we honor God.

A Treasure for Your Thoughts

Consider the following memory verse, and rewrite it in your own words.

Your Memory Treasure . . . .

A man of many companions may come to ruin,
but there is a friend who sticks closer than a
brother.
Proverbs 15:14

In Your Own Words:

Your Creative Space:

Design a Bookmark based on the Proverbs verse.

Journal Your Thoughts

Take a moment to write down your thoughts about today's session.
Here are a few ideas to help you get started:

1. We learned what God says about friendship. Write it in your own words.
2. List some ways you can be a good friend.
3. What are some things you like about your current friends?

Closing Prayer

Dear Lord,
Thank You for the friends we have in our life. Help us grow in love and care for each other just as You have taught us to do. May we always enjoy the times we spend together.
Thank You for this beautiful and unique mother-daughter relationship.
May it bring glory to Your Name and be a light in this world.
In Your Name We Pray,
Amen

Prayer Requests

Are there people in your group who need extra prayers. Is there a world concern that needs to be prayed for? Record them here and pray throughout the week.

A Mother's Reflection . . . . Shared by Julie I.

I remember the moment my first child was born, as most moms do, and the words the doctor uttered, "It's a girl!" I was so excited and hoping for that special mother-daughter bond. A daughter to buy dresses foe, have tea parties with, play dolls with plan a wedding with and have a friend for life!

A year later, my husband and I found out we were pregnant again. What did God have in store for us with baby number two? I had always hoped to have girls close together so they could be friends and sisters. When our second baby arrived, we had another girl. I was over the moon to be blessed with two girls. Girls who I hoped would grow up to be best friends.

My girls are now seventeen and fifteen and I've learned one critical piece of parenting. I've realized throughout the years that they need different parenting. I feel, as I try to be a successful parent to my children, the demands, expectations and scoldings often vary depending on the child and situation. One daughter needs that extra long hug after an altercation; the other needs the last word in our argument. The last word makes her feel she has power over the relationship, but truly, I allow it. Yes, as stubborn as I can be, I will often let her have the last word. Why? As the adult and the more mature of the two, I sometimes will back down from the teenagers. Are we as parents going to call out every eye roll or raised voice or stomping foot? No, I feel the preteens and teens are searching for their autonomy. They are also testing the rules to see what they can get away with in the house.

I realize life is tough and often hormonal with the stress of achieving high grades or meeting new friends, or studying for a test the night before, etc. The one thing I won't negotiate is disrespect. I realize there's often a fine line, but at the end of the day I will not allow my children to disrespect me. I am still the boss. In today's world, the expectations are high on so many levels for our children, but the one place I want them to feel loved, comfortable, and safe is at home with me.

Session 5

The Whole Truth
and Nothing But the Truth . . .

Then you will know the truth and the truth will set you free.

John 8:32

41

Session Overview

We live in a world that sometimes tells us lies about who we are and what we see, but in seeking God's Word, we can find the Truth. We'll look at Bible verses about seeking Truth and how we can look at the world in a different way.

What You'll Need

- Bible
- 3x5 index card and pens for everyone
- Craft supplies (Extending the Session)
- Journal

Opening Prayer

Dear Lord,
Thank You for gathering us here today to have fun and experience Your Word as we seek Your Truth in a world that isn't always what it seems to be. Open our hearts and minds to hear Your Word.
In Your Name We Pray,
Amen

Opening Activity

"Worldly Lies"

Sometimes the world can trick us into believing we need to be or act a certain way to fit in. According to the world's standards, success is measured by what we have, who we are or what we look like, but this is a lie seen and heard everyday on TV, social media, and the radio. So how do we know what to believe?

Just for fun . . . "Three Truths and a Lie"

Each person should have a 3x5 index card and a pen.

Write four statements about yourself: one statement should be false, while three should be true. The goal is to fool people about which one is false. One at a time have each person read her four statements and have the group guess the lie.

(Moms and daughters, try not to give away each other's lie to the group)

Things to Consider

1) What information did you rely on to help you decide which statements were true and which one was the lie?

2) How did it feel to tell the lie?

3) Is it hard to know when you are being lied to? Why/why not?

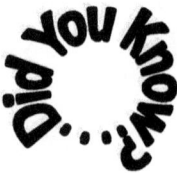

"If you tell the truth, you don't have to remember anything." - Mark Twain

Let's Talk

Consider the words in John 8:31-32.

Fill in the following blanks:

"If you hold to my _____, you are really my _____."

"Then you will know the _____, and the _____

will set you _____."

1) What did Jesus mean in verse 31?

2) What is a disciple?

3) Verse 32 refers to the "Truth."

   What are some ways the "Truth" can set you free?
   (Hint: When we follow God's way of living)

The Biblical Truth . . .

Jesus answered, "I am the way and the truth and the life. No one comes to the Father except through me."

-John 14:6

The dictionary defines truth as "the real facts about something : the things that are true: the quality or state of being true: a statement or idea that is true or accepted as true." We all want to know the truth. Our society relies on telling the truth in order to maintain a system of justice and peace. As Christians, we rely on the Bible to be our source of truth as the living word of God that we can trust and believe in.

Becoming a True Child of God is what we should be working toward and we do this by following Jesus' teachings on how we are to live and what is right. When we follow Jesus, we are free to be all that God meant us to be!

A Treasure for Your Thoughts

Consider the following memory verse, and rewrite it in your own words.

Your Memory Treasure . . . .

Trust in the Lord with all your heart
and lean not on your own understanding;
in all your ways acknowledge him,
and he will make your paths straight.
Proverbs 15:1

In Your Own Words:

Your Creative Space:

Design a Bumper Sticker based on the Proverbs verse.

Journal Your Thoughts

Take a moment to write down your thoughts about today's session.
Here are a few ideas to help you get started:

1. We learned how truth is defined. Write it in your own words.
2. List some things you know to be true.
3. Who are some people you can count on to tell the truth?

Closing Prayer

Dear Lord,
Thank You for the truth You give us through Your Word in the Bible. Help us to live by Your teachings. May we always enjoy these times we spend together learning about each other and Your Word.
Thank you for this beautiful and unique mother-daughter relationship.
May it bring glory to Your Name and be a light in this world.
In Your Name We Pray,
Amen

Prayer Requests

Are there people in your group who need extra prayers? Is there a world concern that needs to be prayed for? Record them here and pray throughout the week.

A Mother's Reflection . . . . Shared by Karen R.

As the world becomes more complicated, sharing a faith journey with my daughter Kiera has taken on a simple and convicting clarity; a relief, but an immense responsibility. My own mother introduced me to a God whose love knows no boundaries and holds no judgment. So as Kiera has grown, it seems only natural that I do the same.

When Kiera turned seven years old and preparing for her First Holy Communion I was given a precious gift. Due to a series of variables, we handled her religious instruction at home as a family. It was a challenge at first, because she didn't have the interaction with her peers and there weren't those fun little crafts to do, but we did our best to make up for the lack in other ways. When she actually received her First Communion, she couldn't have felt more special in the eyes of the community nor in the eyes of God.

Kiera's First Communion gift was a Bible, which she proudly carried with her to Mass each Sunday and read very intentionally. But after two months she suddenly stopped taking it. When asked why, she replied "Mom, it's getting a little boring. I just don't understand why there aren't more girls in the Bible."

Kiera's perspective on her own faith has blossomed into a keen awareness of and deliberate advocacy for the marginalized in her own school as well as in the broader community. She passionately points out injustice and is currently engaged in a formal conversation for community change around racial injustice. My daughter is now often my teacher regarding legitimate faith-related issues.

No doubt God has important plans for Kiera and her passionate commitment to the marginalized. I am honored and blessed to be learning with and from my daughter. It is a gift that has, and will continue, to transform my own spiritual journey.

Session 6

Building a Solid Foundation . . .

"Therefore everyone who hears these words of mine and puts them into practice is like a wise man who built his house on the rock"

Matthew 7:24

Session Overview

Building our lives in Christ Jesus is our one true way to have a firm foundation in the midst of troubles that happens in life. Hearing these words and putting them into practice are two very different things. We'll look at practical ways to put God's Word into action and how that equips us with a solid foundation for life.

What You'll Need

- Bible
- Journal
- Drinking straws (twenty-five per mom/daughter and tape)
- Craft supplies (Extending the Session)

Opening Prayer

Dear Lord,

Thank You for this time You have set aside for us to be together today, so we can gather an understanding about how we are to build a solid foundation in You. Open our hearts that we may experience a fun and fulfilling session.

In Your Name We Pray,

Amen

Opening Activity

"Built to Last"

Have you ever noticed a house being built? The builder starts by laying a foundation for the home to be built upon. If the foundation is done well, the house should withstand cracks in the foundation. If the foundation is not laid well, it can develop cracks over time and essentially ruin the home. A good home is built to last on a solid foundation.

Just for fun . . . "Tall Straw Towers"

Break into mother/daughter teams. Each team should have twenty-five straws and a roll of tape. Allow 10 minutes to see which team can make the tallest self-supporting structure. When the time is up, sit the masterpieces on the floor and see whose structure remains standing the longest . . . that is with a fan blowing or another creative way to mimic wind!

Take a moment to notice . . .

1) What makes one tower stay up longer than another?

2) What made some of them fall quicker?

3) Did the base of the structure help one stay up longer than the others?

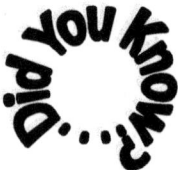

Did you know? . . .

A home's foundation should be checked yearly to make sure it's in good condition. If any problems are detected, they can be corrected.

Let's Talk

Consider the words in Matthew 7:24.

1) What does it mean to put something into practice?

2) Why is it important to build a house on rock or on a solid foundation?

3) As it relates to God's Word, is it more important to hear His word or do what His word says? Explain.

4) When we experience hard times, how do we get through them?

5) What is one thing you can do today that will add to your solid foundation in faith?

Hearing God's Word and Doing God's Work . . .

> *"But everyone who hears these words of mine and does not put them into practice is like a foolish man who built his house on sand."*
>
> **- Matthew 7:26**

1) Why is NOT doing God's work compared to a house built on sand?

2) List some ways to put God's Word into practice: *(Hint: Serving Others)*

It's important to read and hear God's Word, but it's even more important to do what it says. We should spend time studying God's Word in Bible studies, such as this, but what good comes from it if we do not change our behavior or aren't inspired to serve others?

A Solid Foundation of Faith in God's Word is accomplished by following Jesus's teachings on how we are to live. When we follow Jesus, we are free to be all that God meant us to be and will be doing God's work and not just hearing it.

A Treasure for Your Thoughts

Consider the following memory verse, and rewrite it in your own words.

Your Memory Treasure . . . .

Every word of God is flawless; he is a shield to those who take refuge in him.
Proverbs 3:5-6

In Your Own Words:

Your Creative Space:

Design a Button based on the Proverbs verse.

Journal Your Thoughts

Take a moment to write down your thoughts about today's session.
Here are a few ideas to help you get started:
1. What are some ways you can change from studying God's Word?
2. List some things you can do to serve others this week.
3. Write a prayer asking for help in building a solid foundation.

Closing Prayer

Dear Lord,
Thank You for a solid foundation You give us through Your Word in the Bible. Help us to live by Your teachings. May we always enjoy these times we spend together learning about each other and Your Word.
Thank you for this beautiful and unique mother-daughter relationship.
May it bring glory to Your name and be a light in this world.
In Your Name We Pray,
Amen

Prayer Requests

Are there people in your group who need extra prayers? Is there a world concern that needs to be prayed for? Record them here and pray throughout the week.

A Mother's Reflection . . . . Shared by Brenda G.

When I took both our daughters out for the first time on my own, one was four months old and the other four years old. I remember thinking how proud I was to have these two beautiful little creatures in my care like a mother hen gathering her chicks. This seemed easy enough . . . . What could be a more noble calling?

I think about the baptismal promise we made to God and how we are called to care for them, bring them up in the church and nurture their relationship with Christ. Our home was filled with weekly family devotions and we attended church on a regular basis . . . . I felt content we were doing everything we could to fulfill that promise.

As our girls entered the school years, I noticed another kind of influence from outside our home, which sometimes created quite a challenge to help them stay grounded in their faith and to continue down the path we helped shape. My confidence comes from the Lord in raising our girls, but it's also a great reminder that all we can really do is keep praying for them.

Our girls are young adults now, and it's wonderful to see them in new ways outside our home. They are compassionate, caring and thoughtful towards others. The very God who created them is alive inside them through His Holy Spirit, and although they are finding their own faith and reasoning now my daily prayer is that they will come to know the Lord of their youth in an even more meaningful way.

We can pray for our children, keep them safe, get them to church and nurture their faith, but there is no guarantee they will continue to follow God. It is ultimately their choice to discover their own faith on their own terms, but as for me, I will continue to pray daily for the Holy Spirit to reach in and grab hold of them before the world does.

Session 7

Always Say a Prayer . . . ASAP

Do not be anxious about anything, but in everything, by prayer and petition, with thanksgiving, present your requests to God.

Philippians 4:6

Session Overview

There's so much noise going on in the world . . . music, videos, all kinds of electronic devices . . . can leave you feeling anxious. How can anyone hear anything? The answer is prayer! We'll look at the prayer life of Jesus and how He taught us to pray.

What You'll Need

- Bible
- Journal
- Pens, markers and paper
- Craft supplies (Extending the Session)

Opening Prayer

Dear Lord,
Thank You for gathering us here today to have fun and experience Your Word as we explore a prayerful life. Help us to turn our worries into prayers and get to know You better. Open our hearts and minds to hear Your Word.
In Your Name We Pray,
Amen

Opening Activity

"Doodle Bug"
Ever wonder WHY people doodle? Are you a "Doodle Bug"? You probably don't set out to doodle on purpose, but whenever you have a pen in hand the margins of your notebook fill up with little pictures, lines and sometimes even a fancy version of your name outlined with tiny little flowers.

Just for fun . . . "Doodle Prayers"
Each person is given a piece of plain paper, a pen, and some markers.
Allow about 5 - 10 minutes some time to doodle things they are thankful.
(Playing some music that everyone likes can help inspire creativity)

After all have finished, invite each person to show her doodles and end with a "Thanks, God, for . . ." prayer that incorporates each person's name and what she doodled.

Things to Consider

1) When do you doodle and what do you like about doodling?

2) How did you like doodling things you are thankful for?

3) Do you doodle in the margins of your Bible or highlight and underline favorite Scriptures?
   (It's a great way to see where you've been in God's Word)

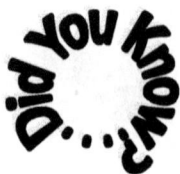

Doodling may actually help you pay attention.
- Jackie Andrade, University of Plymouth

Let's Talk

Consider the words in Joshua Philippians 4:6.

Fill in the following blanks:

Do not be _____ about anything, but in _____,

by _____ and _____, with _____,

present your _____ to God.

1) What sort of things make you anxious?

2) Do you feel like you can go to God in prayer about anything?

3) What does it mean "with thanksgiving" in prayer?

4) What can you pray about today?

Prayerful Consideration . . .

"But when you pray, go into your room, close the door and pray to your Father." **- Matthew 6:7**

"Therefore I tell you, whatever you ask for in prayer, believe that you have received it, and it will be yours." **- Mark 11:24**

1) What do these Bible verses tell us about prayer?

2) What prayer did Jesus teach us to pray? *(Hint: Matthew 6:9)*

It's important to be in prayer with God, because it allows us to build our relationship with Him and helps us align our lives with His will for us. When we go to God with thanksgiving, requests and concerns, He promises to be there with us. Today's readings teach us how to pray and remind us that all things are possible with God!

Prayer Life in Him is also a wonderful way to slow down your busy life and focus on things that matter. Jesus knew He had to make time to get away and pray, and this is what He has taught us to do. Sometimes a prayer can be as simple as one word.

A Treasure for Your Thoughts

Consider the following memory verse, and rewrite it in your own words.

Your Memory Treasure . . . .

Trust in the Lord with all your heart
and lean not on your own understanding;
in all your ways acknowledge him,
and he will make your paths straight.
Proverbs 3:5-6

In Your Own Words:

Your Creative Space:

Design a Bookmark based on the Proverbs verse.

Journal Your Thoughts

Take a moment to write down your thoughts about today's session.
Here are a few ideas to help you get started:
1. List some things that you can pray about.
2. Write a prayer.
3. Doodle.

Closing Prayer

Dear Lord,
Thank You for our time in prayer and study with You. Help us to live by
Your teachings and seek out quiet time with You so we can get to know
You better. Thank you for this beautiful and unique mother-daughter
relationship.
May it bring glory to your name and be a light in this world.
In Your Name We Pray,
Amen

Prayer Requests

Are there people in your group who need extra prayers? Is there a world
concern that needs to be prayed for? Record them here and pray
throughout the week.

A Mother's Reflection . . . . Shared by Dana D.

When I tell people I have two teenage girls, they usually crack a smile and say "I'm sorry." I have to say, having teenagers is not as bad as I would have expected and raising them has been nothing less than a blessing.

We have our challenges. Grades, learning differences, anxiety, social life, self-esteem, and health have all been issues and still are. About a year ago, I had a turning point in my relationship with my children. In order to have the best relationship possible with my family and to help my girls have a happy meaningful life, I needed to change the way I interacted with them. You see, as I began premenopausal it was difficult for me to have a steady disposition. My up and down behavior affected the rhythm of our entire family.

Through a lot of prayer and advice from close family and my doctor, I started changing my focus on the good things that were going on in our lives. Time is taken now to "smell the roses" and show my appreciation for others on a daily basis. Gratitude is the emphasis. I am more open to God's presence in our lives. Sweet gestures resonate deeper, like an "I love you, Mom" spoken from my daughter in the back seat as I drive her to school or an impromptu kiss on the forehead as she walks by me. I thank God for these moments and savor the feeling of joy inside me.

Understanding God's presence in our lives, helps put all the challenges I personally face as a mother into perspective. The seemingly significant becomes insignificant and vice versa. I relish the ability to wake up every morning and say "rise and shine" to my children as my mother said to me and her mother said to her.

Being grateful and showing my gratitude to others has enhanced my relationship with my girls. They have responded well without being aware I purposely changed my approach. Now when we face serious or concerning issues, we try not to be overwhelmed by them, but see them as what makes our family unique. This is who we are; this is our family. Thank you, God!

Session 8

In Thought, Word and Deed . . .

Do not let this Book of the Law depart from your mouth; meditate on it day and night, so that you may be careful to do everything written in it. Then you will be prosperous and successful.

Joshua 1:8

Session Overview

How powerful words can be . . . good or bad! We'll look at the way words can empower and help others. We'll also learn how to THINK before speaking by asking yourself a few simple questions.

What You'll Need

- Bible
- Journal
- Travel size toothpaste for each moms-daughter pair
- Craft supplies (Extending the Session)

Opening Prayer

Dear Lord,
Thank You for gathering us here today to have fun as we explore how powerful words can be. Help us to be mindful of how and when we speak so that what we say may bring others to You. Open our hearts and minds to hear Your Word.
In Your Name We Pray,
Amen

Opening Activity

"Freshen up Your Mouth"
Have you ever said something you wish you could take back? It can happen a lot if we aren't careful with our words – gossip, lies and even swearing. So how do we slow down and learn to be careful with what we say?

A little demonstration . . .

"Toothpaste Tales"
Break into mother/daughter teams. Each team should have a small tube of toothpaste and a ziplock bag. Take a moment to squeeze out the entire tube of paste into the bag.
Now, very carefully, try to put the paste back into the tube.
MISSION IMPOSSIBLE!

Take a moment to notice . . .

No matter how hard you try, you CANNOT put the toothpaste back in the tube. The same thing is true with our words – you cannot put them back in your mouth! Hurtful or harmful words can't be taken back. We need to be really careful about what we say.

One way to stop hurtful words is to "THINK" before you speak:
(Ask yourself these questions)

T . . . . Is it **T**rue?
H . . . . Is it **H**elpful?
I . . . . Is it **I**nspirational?
N . . . . Is it **N**ecessary?
K . . . . Is it **K**ind?

Did you know?...

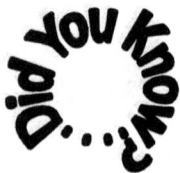

Whoever gossips to you will gossip about you.

- Spanish Proverb

Let's Talk

Consider the words in Joshua 1:8.

Fill in the following blanks:

Do not let this _____ depart from your mouth; _____ on it day and night, so that you may be careful to do everything written in it. Then you will be _____ and successful.

1) Why do you think the Bible is referred to as the Book of the Law?

2) What does it mean to meditate on something?

3) How can following God's Law make us prosperous and successful?

4) How does following God's Law free us up to live?

5) How do you define successful?

Building Each Other Up . . .

Do not let any unwholesome talk come out of your mouths, but only what is helpful for building others up according to their needs.

- Ephesians 4:29

1)   What is meant by unwholesome talk?

2)   How can we build others up with our words?

We live in a fast-paced world with an endless supply of instant information through our phones, computers and TVs. Words stream in and out like water and not always in an inspirational or helpful way, so we need to slow down and be aware of what we are seeing and hearing.

We need to be intentional with our words in a way that is helpful to others. We can start by putting down our phones, turn off the TV and walk away from our computers, so we can acknowledge the people around us. In this instant, our actions will speak louder than words.

Words Have the Power to uplift others. When we take the time to encourage others, we honor our relationship with them and in doing so, we honor God.

A Treasure for Your Thoughts

Consider the following memory verse, and rewrite it in your own words.

Your Memory Treasure . . . .

Reckless words pierce like a sword,
but the tongue of the wise brings healing.
Proverbs 12:18

In Your Own Words:

Your Creative Space:

Design a Bumper Sticker based on the Proverbs verse.

Journal Your Thoughts

Take a moment to write down your thoughts about today's session. Here are a few ideas to help you get started:

1. List some ways you can use your words for good.
2. Review ideas.
3. Write a letter of encouragement to someone.

Closing Prayer

Dear Lord,

Thank You for Your written Word in the Bible. Help us use our words to uplift each other. Thank You for this beautiful and unique mother-daughter relationship.

May it bring glory to Your Name and be a light in this world.

In Your Name We Pray,

Amen

Prayer Requests

Are there people in your group who need extra prayers? Is there a world concern that needs to be prayed for? Record them here and pray throughout the week.

A Mother's Reflection . . . . Shared by Amy K.

I grew up in a Christian home and have many fond memories of my mom raising me. What I remember the most is she was always there and willing to listen or help with whatever I needed. It didn't matter if it was "her time" to read in bed before falling asleep, I was never made to feel like she didn't have time for me. She was very patient and loving. I know I didn't appreciate all she did for me at the time but, as an adult with my own children, I now realize the wonderful gift she gave me.

The values and love she gave me as a child have formed me into the adult I am today and I believe that the older I get the closer the bond between us becomes. My greatest hope is that I can provide my own daughter with the same love and patience I was provided with as a child. My daughter is six years old and we adopted her when she was two years old. I love her as much as if I were her birth mother.

After having three sons and then a daughter, I can see how it is a very different relationship. I hope to look back someday and see how I have formed my daughter, and I look forward to watching our relationship grow as we grow together. No one said being a parent was easy but it's definitely rewarding. With God's help, we can make it through all situations.

Session 9

When We Worship . . .

Let everything that has breath praise the Lord. Praise the Lord.

Psalm 150:6

Session Overview

The world around us is a beautiful reminder of God's creation – the mountains, trees, flowers, animals. We'll consider the way we look at the world and how everything we do can be a form of worship when it is God-centered.

What You'll Need

- Bible
- Journal
- Paper or poster boards, colored pencils and/or markers
- Craft supplies (Extending the Session)

Opening Prayer

Dear Lord,
Thank You for gathering us here today. Help us to see the beauty in the world around us and to know You are the Creator. Help us tell others about You, so they will want to sing Your praises as well.
In Your Name We Pray,
Amen

Opening Activity

"Creative Worship"
Have you ever considered when you see beauty in nature and shout out a thanks to God that this is a form of worship? Well, it is, but do you know why? It's God-centered and you are focusing on the Creator's beauty!

A little creation . . . "A Picture is Worth a Thousand Words"
Break into mother-daughter teams. Each team should have a piece of butcher paper or poster board and colored pencils or markers. Allow 15-20 minutes to draw and/or write out responses of what God means to them. Your project can be artwork, one word, song lyrics or prayers. Get creative in your team creation!

Take a moment to share . . .

After the time is up, go around the room and share your creation as a team. Isn't it great to be inspired by others' creations about God?

Things to notice:

How are the projects similar?

How are they different?

Isn't it fun to get creative about God?

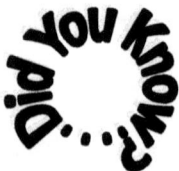

Did you know?...

> **Worship is about coming into God's presence.**
> **- Jack Hayford**

Let's Talk

Please read all of Psalm 150.

Consider the following:

(The "Who, What, Where, and How" of Praise and Worship!)

1) Who is supposed to praise God?

2) What are we supposed to praise Him for?

3) Where are we supposed to worship Him?

4) How are we supposed to worship Him?

Worshipful Thinking . . .

Do not let any unwholesome talk come out of your mouths, but only what is helpful for building others up according to their needs.   **- Ephesians 4:29**

Think of ways we can use our senses to worship God:

Sight

Hearing

Touch

Smell

Taste

The Oxford dictionary defines worship two ways.

1. Noun – The feeling or expression of reverence and adoration for a deity: "the worship of God."
2. Verb – Show reverence and adoration for a deity; honor with religious rites: "the Maya built jungle pyramids to worship their gods."

Consider the ways we use our senses to worship that you came up with and imagine if we only thought of worship as a noun and not a verb. Because of our reverence (noun) for God, one way we put our faith and worship into action (verb) is by serving others.

Worship the Lord with all your senses so that others may come to know God through you. Worship is also a time for you to give thanks and praise to God!

A Treasure for Your Thoughts

Consider the following memory verse, and rewrite it in your own words.

Your Memory Treasure . . . .

Let love and faithfulness never leave you;
bind them around your neck,
write them on the table of your heart.
Proverbs 3:3

In Your Own Words:

Your Creative Space:

Design a Button based on the Proverbs verse.

Journal Your Thoughts

Take a moment to write down your thoughts about today's session.
Here are a few ideas to help you get started:
1. List some ways you can use your senses to worship.
2. What is your favorite way or place to worship?
3. Have you ever invited someone to worship with you?

Closing Prayer

Dear Lord,
Thank You for the gift of worship and the many ways You call us into worship with You. May we always enjoy these times we spend together learning about each other and Your Word.
Thank You for this beautiful and unique mother-daughter relationship.
May it bring glory to Your Name and be a light in this world.
In Your Name We Pray,
Amen

Prayer Requests

Are there people in your group who need extra prayers? Is there a world concern that needs to be prayed for? Record them here and pray throughout the week.

A Daughter's Reflection . . . . Shared by Laney

How Do I love thee? Let me count the ways . . .
You are better than a crisp book on a winter's day.
I'd rather be with you than in the library.
Your love is greater than the universe.

You are like the glue in my life that binds the pages of my life.

You're as beautiful as a blooming rose.

You are as warm as orange tea during a blizzard.

You're as loving as a cuddly puppy.

Your soft touch is like a fleece blanket.

I'd rather be with you than Harry Potter.

Your cooking is like heaven.

Your voice is like a beautiful song.

These are the ways I love thee.

Love, Laney

Age 10

Session 10

A Forgiving Heart . . .

Be kind and compassionate to one another, forgiving each other, just as in Christ God forgave you.

Ephesians 4:32

Session Overview

It may feel easier to stay mad at someone rather than forgive them, but we need to remember that we suffer inside when we don't forgive. We'll explore what it means to truly forgive and how that empowers us to be kind and compassionate toward others.

What You'll Need

- Bible
- Journal
- Balloons: (not blown up) One for each person
- Craft supplies (Extending the Session)

Opening Prayer

Dear Lord,
Thank You for gathering us here today. Help us to understand what it means to forgive others and what we can learn from true forgiveness. Open our hearts and minds to hear Your Word and to enjoy this time together.
In Your Name We Pray,
Amen

Opening Activity

"Let It Go"

What is forgiveness? It means letting go of the feelings you have toward someone who has hurt you or disappointed you in some way, so you can move forward and get on with life. It doesn't mean we aren't hurt by someone, but we are willing to forgive and give them another chance. When we harbor bad feelings toward others, we become bitter and unable to move forward with relationships.

"Let Those Feelings Out"

What are some of the feelings you have when someone does something hurtful to you? Recognizing and letting go of those feelings is part of forgiving someone and how we move on in a healthy way.

Balloons Away . . . . Everyone should have a balloon (not blown up) Read the following statements out loud. Inflate or deflate your balloon as instructed:

- You keep your angry feelings inside when someone hurts you.
  Inflate your balloon halfway.
- You forgive that person who hurt you.
  Deflate your balloon all the way.
- You stay angry at someone and never tell them why.
  Inflate your balloon half way.
- Someone hurts you and you avoid them.
  Inflate your balloon completely full, but hold on to it.

As you hold your inflated balloon, think about how it feels to hold on to those bad feelings that fill you with anger and resentment.
Now release the balloon into the air. Notice how the out-of-control balloon flies around. When we keep our feelings in and never let them go, we may end up as out of control.

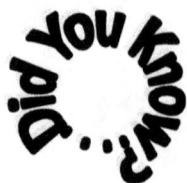

> There is no love without forgiveness and there is no forgiveness without love.
> - Bryant H. McGill

Let's Talk

Please read Ephesians 4:31-32.

Consider the following:

1) What is meant by: "Get rid of all bitterness"?

2) What are some other things we are supposed to get rid of?

3) How are we supposed to be with each other?

4) Why should we forgive others?

5) Is there someone you have trouble forgiving?

God is Forgiving . . .

Gladden the soul of your servant, for to you, O lord, do I lift up my sou. For you, O Lord, are good and forgiving, abounding in steadfast love to all who call upon you.   **- Psalm 86:4-5**

Our God is a kind and loving God. We can go to Him anytime in prayer and know our sins are forgiven; because Jesus was sent here to die on the cross for our sins. What a loving act to do on our behalf!

So what does this have to do with forgiving others? Well, because God loved us first and out of that response, we should love others . . . part of that is forgiving each other because God forgives us.

The Power of Forgiveness means we have the power of the Holy Spirit within us to truly love and forgive others, because that's what God first did for us. When we forgive, we are reacting to God's love for us and are free to love others.

A Treasure for Your Thoughts

Consider the following memory verse, and rewrite it in your own words.

Your Memory Treasure . . . .

He who covers over an offense promotes love,
but whoever repeats the matter
separates close friends.

Proverbs 12:18

In Your Own Words:

Your Creative Space:

Design a Bookmark based on the Proverbs verse.

Journal Your Thoughts

Take a moment to write down your thoughts about today's session.
Here are a few ideas to help you get started:

1. Write a prayer asking God to always help you forgive others.
2. What are some things you can ask God to forgive you for?
3. Make a list of how we should be toward others.

Closing Prayer

Dear Lord,
Thank You for loving us so much that You sent Jesus here to die for our sins. Help us to show others Your love by our actions toward them.
Thank You for this beautiful and unique mother-daughter relationship.
May it bring glory to Your Name and be a light in this world.
In Your Name We Pray,
Amen

Prayer Requests

Are there people in your group who need extra prayers? Is there a world concern that needs to be prayed for? Record them here and pray throughout the week.

A Mother's Reflection . . . . Shared by Laura S.

Nora was born with a severe congenital heart defect: one of the four chambers of her heart never developed. To have any chance at life, she needed a series of three heart surgeries, the first when she was only two weeks old. It was a time of mixed emotions – joy at the birth of our first daughter, but confusion, fear and sadness at the path that lay ahead, and the uncertainty of her life. I was afraid. Would I be up for the job of being a mother?

We did not know what to expect those first days of Nora's life, but we knew her life would be centered in the One who gives life, Jesus Christ. We chose to have her baptized at home when she was just five days old. Our family gathered around the dining room table one Sunday after church. Her baptismal gown was from her father's baptism thirty years before. The baptismal water came from her great-grandmother who, though too frail to travel, had filled a glass bottle with water, said a blessing over it and entrusted relatives to bring it to us. My father-in-law, a pastor, performed the ceremony. Taking our beautiful wee girl in his big hands and holding her tight, he said, "I baptize you in the name of the Father, and of the Son, and of the Holy Spirit."

At that moment, I felt the responsibility of being a mother in a new way. I felt strongly my husband and I were not alone but that our whole family was taking part in the raising of this child whether her life be brief or long. God Himself called Nora His own and loved her far more than ever I could. Christ, our Savior and our Healer, would be with Nora through all that lay ahead. His love surrounded her. My task as a mother was to point out His love to her every day of her life – to show Christ to her that she might come to feel His presence, too.

Five years later, Nora is thriving. She has a big scar on her chest as a reminder of all she has been through. The challenges of mothering have now moved from life-and-death moments to packing lunches and finding clean clothes for church. I still give thanks daily that I am not alone in raising this creative, smart, beautiful little girl. She is first and foremost a child of God.

Session 11

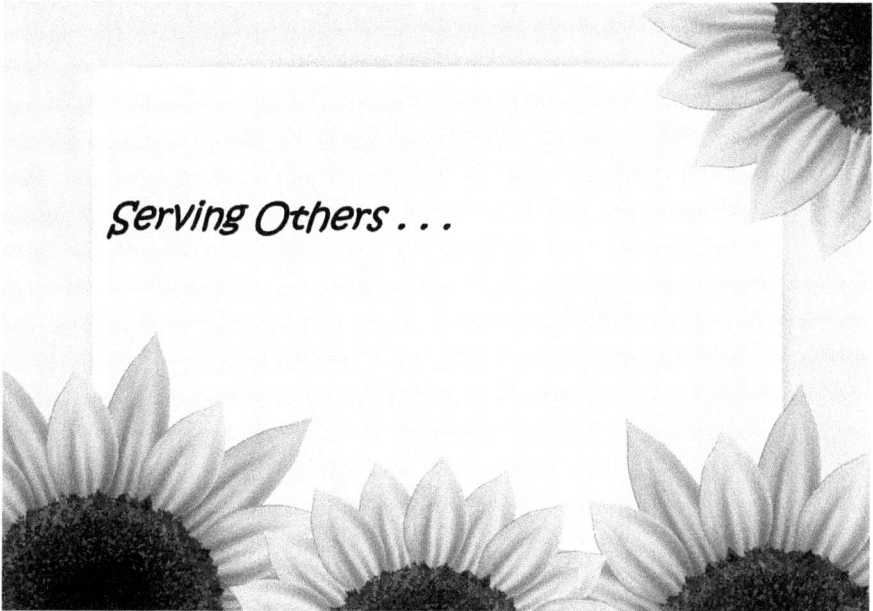

Serving Others . . .

Each one should use whatever gift he has received to serve others, faithfully administering God's grace in its various forms.

1 Peter 4:10

Session Overview

God has given each of us special gifts to serve others, and through our service we convey God's loving grace. We'll look at ways we can use our gifts at any age or any stage of our faith journey.

What You'll Need

- Bible
- Journal
- Pens, paper and poster board
- Craft supplies (Extending the Session)

Opening Prayer

Dear Lord,
Thank You for gathering us here today to experience Your Word and have fun as we explore serving others. Help us to discover our gifts that will lead us to serving others. Open our hearts and minds to hear Your Word.
In Your Name We Pray,
Amen

Opening Activity

"Serving Others"

God has given each of us specific gifts we can use to serve others in our daily lives. Where do we begin to look for ways we can serve? Let's start by looking at the needs of others first.

Take a Moment:

Everyone should have a pen and paper. Take five minutes to allow everyone to write down ideas of how to serve in the following categories:

Home

Community

Church

School

Share these ideas out loud as a group . . .

As each of you share your ideas, have someone record them on a poster board under each category.

What are some ideas you can do today?

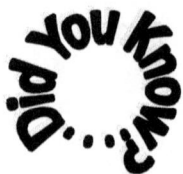

Did you know?...

Serving others is a spiritual discipline.

Let's Talk

Please read 1 Peter 4:10 and fill in the blanks:

Each one should use whatever _____ he has _____ to

_____ others, faithfully administering God's _____ in its

various _____.

    1)   What do you think is meant by gifts?
        (Hint: Your abilities)

    2)   What gifts can we use to serve others?

    3)   Why does Scripture mention "in its various forms"?
        (Hint: Ways we can serve)

    4)   What are some gifts you see in others?

Serving Others . . .

For even the Son of Man came not to be served but to serve.

- Mark 10:45

There are several ways we can serve others, but how do we truly find which way is best suited for our gifts? How can we know? When we start listening to where God is leading us to serve, we will find our way. Determining God's plan for us starts with a consistent prayer life. When we are in tune with what God is revealing to us, we will see the needs of others and can take action.

So why is it so important to serve others? God sent Jesus here to show us how to live, and he modeled how important it is to serve others. Jesus came to serve. If you really look around, you will find ways to serve. It may be within your own family or home, or by simply helping out when needed.

To Serve Others with a Kind Heart means we see a need and find a way to do what is necessary without expecting anything in return.

There are always ways to serve, so when we are ready, willing, and able, we can make a difference in the world around us.

A Treasure for Your Thoughts

Consider the following memory verse, and rewrite it in your own words.

Your Memory Treasure . . . .

A generous person will prosper;
whoever refreshes others will be refreshed.

In Your Own Words:

Your Creative Space:

Design a Bumper Sticker based on the Proverbs verse.

Journal Your Thoughts

Take a moment to write down your thoughts about today's session.
Here are a few ideas to help you get started:
1. Make a list of ways you can serve others in your home.
2. What are some ways you can serve others today?
3. What are some ways you can make a difference in the world?

Closing Prayer

Dear Lord,
Thank You for loving us so much that You sent Jesus here to show us how we can serve others. Help us to show others Your love by our actions.
Thank You for this beautiful and unique mother-daughter relationship.
May it bring glory to Your Name and be a light in this world.
In Your Name We Pray,
Amen

Prayer Requests

Are there people in your group who need extra prayers? Is there a world concern that needs to be prayed for? Record them here and pray throughout the week.

A Mother's Reflection . . . . Shared by Kathy D.

"Hand M.A.D.E. with Love"
My fondest memories of childhood are not of my mom singing me to sleep, but rather peacefully drifting off to sleep to the rhythmic lullaby of her sewing machine. Mom is a seamstress as were her mother and grandmother before her.

Christmas was always extra special because the gifts didn't come from a store, but from Mom's sewing room and always had a label that read "Hand Made with Love". Every time she made me a new outfit, she made sure that my "fashion doll" had an exact duplicate.

When the time was right, she lovingly passed on to me her knowledge of the genteel arts of sewing, knitting, crocheting and needlework as her mother had to her. I cherished that special time we spent together so many years ago.

Before long, I was a mom continuing the tradition and teaching my own daughter Maggie to sew, crochet and knit. Fast forward twenty years. Maggie is now an accomplished knitter. Yesterday she sent me a text with an attachment showing a pair of beautiful blue gloves. The text read:
"What do you think of the color? I'm knitting them for Grandma for Christmas."

Session 12

Be the Light in the World . . .

You are the light of the world. A city on a hill cannot be hidden.

Matthew 5:14

Session Overview

What does it mean to be a light in the world? We'll look at ways we can be a positive influence, a reflection of the love of Christ Jesus and a light in the world.

What You'll Need

- Bible
- Journal
- Pens, paper and poster board
- Craft supplies (Extending the Session)

Opening Prayer

Dear Lord,
Thank You for gathering us here today to experience Your Word and have fun as we explore what it means to be a light in the world. Help us understand how we can reflect God's love. Open our hearts and minds to hear Your Word.
In Your Name We Pray,
Amen

Opening Activity

"The Light Way"
When we live as Christ taught us to live, we light the way for others to follow Him. We are a light in the world that shines in the darkness.

Take a Moment:
Separate the daughters and their moms by having each group meet in a separate room. Have someone record the "Group Discussion" notes to be shared later.

Discuss the following:

1) Flip through all the chapters of this book and assign one word for each.

2) What does it mean to be a light in the world?

3) Write a brief explanation of why following Christ will help you become a light in the world.

"Putting it all Together"
Come back together as a large group and share your answers to the three discussion questions. Develop a summary for questions (2) and (3) and record each summary on a poster board. Then read the summaries out loud to reinforce what we've been learning throughout this study together.

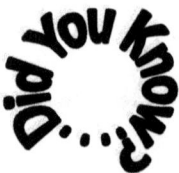

Did you know?...

> All the darkness in the world cannot extinguish the light of a single candle.
> - Francis of Assisi

Let's Talk

Please read Matthew 5:14-16.

Consider the following:

1) Who does Jesus say is the light of the world?

2) Where are we supposed to be in order for our light to be seen?
   (Hint: vs. 16)

3) What will our light reveal to others?

4) What are some ways in which we hide our light?
   (Hint: The opposite of how we help others in need)

5) Is there someone you know who could use Jesus's light?

Light My Way . . .

Your word is a lamp to my feet and a light for my path.
- Psalm 119:105

God is happy and excited for us when we take what we are learning and apply it to our lives. God gave us Jesus Christ so that we could learn from Him and reflect His love to others. When we consider all we have learned together through this study and begin living our lives accordingly, we are free to love and live in His will for us.

So what does this mean for our lives? God sent Jesus here to show us how to live and He gave us a purpose for our lives. We each have a unique gift that will help us serve others and reflect God's love.

You Are a Special Light who reflects God's love to others. How special do you feel right now? We have been given a special gift, and we are commissioned to share that gift with everyone! Our life is our work for God when we choose to share it. With God's help, we can make a difference in the world around us.

A Treasure for Your Thoughts

Consider the following memory verse, and rewrite it in your own words.

Your Memory Treasure . . . .

The path of the righteous is like the first gleam of
dawn, shining ever brighter till the full light of day.

Proverbs 12:18

In Your Own Words:

Your Creative Space:

Design a Button based on the Proverbs verse.

Journal Your Thoughts

Take a moment to write down your thoughts about today's session.
Here are a few ideas to help you get started:
1. What can you do better to be a reflection of God's love?
2. What are some things you can do today to be a light?
3. What are some ways you can make a difference in the world?

Closing Prayer

Dear Lord,
Thank You for loving us so much that You sent Jesus here to show us how we are to live. Help us to reflect Your love by our actions, so we can be the light in the world that leads others to You.
Thank You for this beautiful and unique mother-daughter relationship.
May it bring glory to Your Name and be a light in this world.
In Your Name We Pray,
Amen

Prayer Requests

Are there people in your group who need extra prayers? Is there a world concern that needs to be prayed for? Record them here and pray throughout the week.

A Granddaughter's Reflection . . . . Shared by Brenda G.

Summers for me meant visiting my grandma on a huge farm near the boot heel of Missouri. My cousins and I had free range of the farm to roam, get caught up in the beauty of nature – trees, wildflowers, creeks full of crayfish, tall grassy fields – and explore from sun up to sun down. Looking back, I believe Grandma's farm was my little piece of heaven on earth.

Grandma always had chores for me when I was there. I collected the eggs, pitched the hay, washed dishes and, when the garden was ready, picked the vegetables. She read to me from the Bible every night as I worked on snapping the peas for our dinner. It was as if God were speaking the words through her as she read. I loved her dearly.

I remember, as a young child, having a deep connection with God especially through my prayer life. I think, much like my Grandma's garden, seeds had been planted in me – seeds of faith. My parents modeled for me how to get down on my knees and pray. We prayed for meals, well-being, thanksgiving, praise and for others in need. I was shown that I could go to God in prayer for anything and I did! They laid a foundation of faith for my life's journey.

Train a child in the way he should go and when he is old he will not turn from it.
Proverbs 22:6

I am so thankful for the legacy of faith in our family, especially over the last two generations from my grandma to my mom and now for me, the third generation, to plant the seeds of faith for my own daughters.

Four generations of faith.

Although my daughters never had the opportunity to meet my Grandma in this world, her legacy of faith is still very much alive!

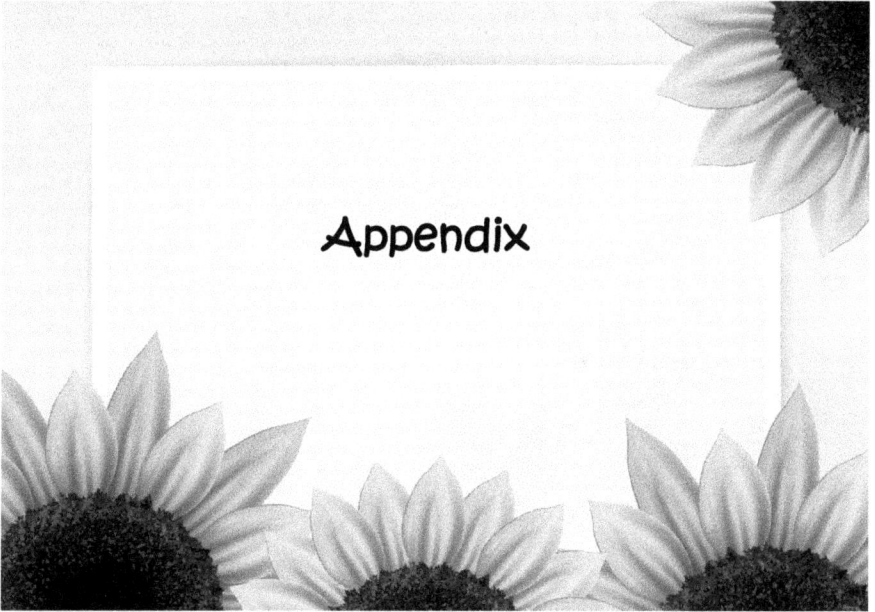

Appendix

Leader's Notes

Leading this study is simply about encouraging others to participate in the activities and discussions. If this is your first time to lead or facilitate a group study, you may feel both nervous and excited. But no worries! This study is proven to be a useful tool to get moms and daughters talking and engaging in lively discussions.

Your leadership is a gift, but keep in mind that other group members can take on active roles as well. You can divide up sessions, activities and/or discussions among members. Each meeting should last an hour which is perfect for even the busiest moms. Schedule a regular day to meet monthly or weekly, and always start and end on time. The main idea is to get the group together regularly and to keep them together for the twelve sessions.

Some suggestions for great small group meetings:

1) Create a 'SAFE" Environment
   S – Seek Connection
   A – Accept One Another
   F – Focus on Fun
   E – Encourage Each Other
2) Keep It Simple
   Group size should be twelve or less, so everyone can get to know each other and build relationships:
   To Know and Be Known
   To Love and Be Loved
   To Serve and Be Served
   To Celebrate and Be Celebrated
3) Always Begin and End in Prayer . . .
   Invite God in!
4) Reflect after Meetings
   Consider the following questions:
   ✓ Did you enjoy the meeting?
   ✓ What went well?
   ✓ Did everyone participate?
   ✓ What would you do differently next time?

Extending the Sessions

Lingering a bit longer after a meeting can be fun. Consider adding a craft to go along with a session. Depending on the season, you can also make gifts or put together gift baskets. It takes extra effort, but with internet access you can search "How-To" for any kind of craft or project. Remember to ask members of the group to help gather the necessary supplies needed so that task doesn't always fall on one person.

Some Suggestions for Added Fun to Each Session:

Session 1 – Make a beaded cross necklace.

Session 2 – Create a magnetic locker mirror and decorate.

Session 3 – Decorate a small frame with a picture of your family in it.

Session 4 – Make friendship bracelets.

Session 5 – Create one-of-a-kind bookmarks with Scripture on them.

Session 6 – Make a paperweight.

Session 7 – Make prayer beads to keep or give away.

Session 8 – Create positive magnetic messages for the refrigerator.

Session 9 – Create personalized door knob hangers for your family.

Session 10 – Create stationery with Scripture on the inside.

Session 11 – Create gift baskets filled with seasonal items.

Session 12 – Make homemade candles in mason jars.

Celebrate, Serve and Retreat

Celebrate

When your group has made it through at least six sessions, be sure to celebrate your accomplishment! Make it a special occasion by bringing extra goodies to share and acknowledging each other. A good old-fashioned cookie exchange is always a favorite pastime!

Serve

When the group finishes Session 11, take the opportunity to plan a service project together. It's a great way to share God's love and to be a light in the world!

Retreat

Take time to get away with your group, even if it's only for half-a-day at your church or local retreat center. A retreat refreshes the mind, rejuvenates the spirit and creates a stronger mother-daughter bond through faith.

To get started on planning, pick a theme based on one of the sessions and build from there. For example: Session 4 on "Friends" can be a day centered on how to be a good friend and how friends can hold each other accountable. Invite a youth leader or pastor to lead a simple worship and/or lead the Bible study and group discussion.

A SAMPLE DAY RETREAT SCHEDULE:

9:00 am	Continental Breakfast
9:30	Worship (Led by Youth Leader or Pastor)
10:15	Opening Activity
10:45	Break
11:00	Bible Study & Discussion
12:00	Lunch (Keep it simple)
1:00	Make and Take Craft or Service Project
2:00	Closing Prayer & Dismissal

About the Author

Brenda S. Gibson is an energetic, Christ-centered writer, speaker and leader with proven ability to create, write and implement programs that are current and inspirational. She has written Christian curriculum, synod-wide publications, poignant liturgy and marketing materials.

Brenda is a wife of 30+ years and a mother of two young adult daughters and thoroughly enjoys their engaging conversations.

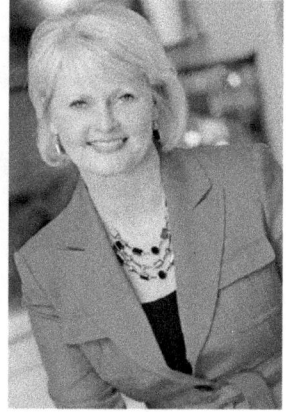

She believes all things are possible with God.

"That I may publish with the voice of thanksgiving, and tell of all thy wondrous works."
- Psalm 26:7

Connect with Brenda

Email	Brensgibson@gmail.com
Blog	Madebybrendagibson.blogspot.com
Facebook	Brenda Gibson
Twitter	Brenda S. Gibson
LinkedIn	Brenda Gibson
Website	Madebybrendagibson.com

INVITE ME TO SPEAK AT YOUR NEXT EVENT . . .

www.ingramcontent.com/pod-product-compliance
Lightning Source LLC
Chambersburg PA
CBHW060303050426
42448CB00009B/1734